The cross where all roads meet

The cross
where all roads meet

César Malan

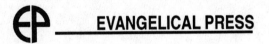 **EVANGELICAL PRESS**

EVANGELICAL PRESS
12 Wooler Street, Darlington, Co. Durham, DL1 1RQ, England

First published in French under the title *La Vraie Croix*
(original edition 1831, modernized version published by
Europresse sarl, 1993).
This translation first published 1994
© Evangelical Press 1994

British Library Cataloguing in Publication Data available

ISBN 0 85234 316 7

Printed and bound in Great Britain at the Bath Press, Avon.

Contents

The true cross

1.
A meeting by a cross

Not far from St Laurent, on one of the most beautiful peaks of the Jura, stands an old cross. It is set close by a wood of beech and fir trees, at a point where several paths meet.

This decaying monument to a love which will never end ought to remind everyone who sees it of the eternal sacrifice of the Son of God. It focuses our thoughts on all that the Crucified One obtained for his church at such great cost. But how few really understand the true message of the cross, this token of redemption! How few even of those who bear the name of Christians are moved by the sight of the memorial to the Saviour's death to love the Lamb of God who was slain and hung on the cross!

The reaction of many to the sight of the cross to which the Holy and Righteous One was nailed is rather to 'shoot out the lip … [and] shake the head' and become even more hardened in their unbelief.

Then again, there are many who do indeed call on the name of the Son of God, but who have been led astray by prejudice or ignorance. They seek from the worthless, dead wood of an earthly cross what can only be found in the Saviour who, it is true, died on that tree of shame, but is now alive and exalted to the Father's glory.

When the people of Israel were perishing in the desert as a result of the bites of the fiery serpents, Moses, acting on God's command, raised up a bronze serpent on a pole. As God had promised, everyone who looked towards this symbol was immediately healed. The Israelites turned their eyes towards the serpent, but in doing so they were really looking to the power of God and the deliverance that came from him. This object which had been cast in metal represented for the believer something very different from what superstition made of it afterwards! In the camp in the desert the bronze serpent proclaimed the promise and the mercy of God. Seven centuries later, however, this lump of bronze had become an idol. Israel burned incense to it and even those who had turned away from the Lord worshipped the symbol rather than the Benefactor!

Jesus, the one beloved by the Father, was lifted up on a cross. The promise is made once more that all who in faith look on this victim will be healed of their wounds and saved from the death which their sin deserves. The believer looks to Jesus and takes hold of the promise. The ignorant and the idolator burn incense to a cross and, though they bend the knee before an outward symbol, they forget and even reject the one whom it is meant to commemorate!

Such were the thoughts passing through my mind as I rested my tired body on the lush carpet of grass at the foot of the cross. I had just crossed over the mountain and was regaining my strength before continuing on to the place where I was to spend the night, which was still some distance away. As I sat there, I reflected on this great God and Saviour whom the Christian can meet with anywhere, up in the mountains or down on the plain, in solitude or in the company of other believers.

'O Holy Spirit,' I said in my soul, 'lift up my heart to my Father! O Jesus, my Shepherd, look down on one of your sheep who is calling on you! Let me hear your voice speaking gentle words of peace and hope!'

At that moment two peasants went past, followed by an old man whose outward appearance seemed to indicate that he belonged to the upper classes. The countrymen raised their hats, crossed themselves and went on their way. The old man stopped, took off his hat in a gesture of respect and bowed his white head before the cross.

'O Lord,' I prayed inwardly, 'have pity on this soul! If he does not know the true cross on which you died, oh, give me an opportunity to show him your grace!'

2.

The traveller's religion

His prayers at an end, the old man replaced his hat. Leaning on his stick with both hands, he greeted me cordially and asked if I was a traveller and if I had come far.

'I am just walking in the mountains,' I replied. 'But all the same, I am a traveller, for we are all travelling towards eternity, and we are very near our journey's end.'

The old man stood looking at me in silence, as if trying to fathom out what sort of man this was who answered him in so serious a manner. Then, sitting down in front of me by the side of the path, he asked cautiously, 'May I ask you what your religion is?'

'The religion of heaven,' I stated plainly. 'The one which the only begotten Son of God himself brought us, and which he sealed for all eternity when he shed his blood on a gibbet like this one.'

I seem to have aroused the old man's interest even more by this latest reply. I could see that he was pondering carefully what he should say to me and that he was turning over a number of thoughts in his mind.

'May I ask,' he said at last, rather abruptly, 'if you are a Roman Catholic or … a Protestant?'

'I know only one name,' I answered courteously, 'under heaven, given among men, whereby we must be saved. This great and lovely name is that of Jesus Christ, the Son of God, and I call myself by this name alone. I am a Christian.'

These words seemed to embarrass the old man somewhat. Smiling, as if he was afraid of admitting he had said something wrong, he told me, 'I too bear this name, for I too believe that the Lord Jesus Christ died for me on this cross. At least, … I hope so.'

'A hope is very little to go on,' I replied gravely, 'when it is a matter of life or death. Uncertainty, or even the smallest doubt on this subject, is a very serious matter. At any moment we could find there is no more time left for searching or for waiting for an answer. How awful it will be when the Bridegroom himself tells the foolish virgins who did not take any oil in their lamps: "The door is shut and I do not know you"!' (Matt. 25:1-12).

'You are very solemn,' said the old man, passing his hand across his forehead, 'but what you say interests me a great deal. Can we talk some more on this subject? I

13

must confess that it is something I think about quite often.'

If you who are reading this love the Lord Jesus, you will appreciate what a joy it was to me when he made this request. So I answered the old man: 'What better use could we make of this hour which God has given us than to spend it in reflecting on the wonderful love he has shown us in his holy Son Jesus? There is nothing I like better, I assure you, than to talk about the things of heaven. Since we both have the same desire, may it please the Lord to guide our conversation by the Spirit of truth and love!'

'Amen!' he added, clasping both his hands against his chest. 'May God be pleased to do so! And may he let me hear from your mouth words of peace and comfort for my soul.'

3.

What the old man believed

'Do you feel the need for peace and comfort, then?' I asked.

'Yes, I need both. I want peace with God and my heart is still troubled over a number of things.'

'Surely the things that have to do with eternity are more important to you than those that only concern this world? Troubles and difficulties are nothing compared with the soul's fears about the future.'

'That is indeed true,' he agreed, 'for, as you have said, eternity is very near us.'

'And does the thought of approaching it make you tremble?' I asked, in the hope that he would open his heart to me.

He answered me with the most agreeable frankness: 'As you are being so kind in giving me so much of your attention, sir, I will tell you all my thoughts on this subject. I admit, I am very worried about my salvation.

The fact that I am seventy-six years old means that I think about it every day. Since I believe the Holy Scriptures, I do not make light of what comes after death. I desire above all else to have divine grace.

'My life has been a varied one. My birth and my natural preferences led me into the hustle and bustle of the world and kept me there for many years. I grew tired of it all, and for the last ten years I have led a very quiet life. In this retirement I have devoted most of my time to the search for what the one who cannot err calls "the one thing that is needed".'

'The very fact that you desire this grace, without which no one will see God, is in itself a great blessing,' I said. 'You will know a much greater blessing if you lay hold of it by faith so that it becomes yours now.'

'It is no light matter,' the old man assured me, 'and it takes a great deal of effort to obtain it. But, however hard work it may be, I am not without hope of achieving it. Other sinners have managed it, so why shouldn't I too be able to earn this grace?'

It was when he said this that I knew that this interesting man was still in ignorance about the grace of God. The gift of the Father through Jesus Christ had not yet been revealed to him. He had indeed used the beautiful word 'grace', but he did not understand the meaning of it, as he had talked of earning it. He obviously regarded salvation as a blessing which he could acquire by means of hard work and effort.

16

I wanted to be sure that this was indeed what he thought, so I asked him if he thought he was near his goal, or if he was afraid that he was still a long way off it.

'It isn't right for any sinner to boast,' he replied humbly, 'and for me least of all. But despite my great weakness, may I not hope that this good God, who calls himself love and who speaks of himself as a tender Father, will have pity on me, and on my ignorance and, alas, my misery? And — dare I say it? — will he perhaps be content with what I have been able to do, or at least have wanted to do, to gain his favour?'

These words left me in no doubt as to the spiritual state of my companion. His confession of faith was unequivocal. He expected to receive the forgiveness of his sins and acceptance into heaven as a reward for his works — a magnificent reward, certainly, but none the less one that had been earned, at least in part, by a series of good works and sacrifices.

Perhaps you, dear reader, are asking whether he was right, after all. Is it not up to the sinner to seek for God's forgiveness? Can he not be said to have earned it when, having turned away from evil, he makes up for his earlier misdeeds by good behaviour and leads an upright life? Is God's justice more uncompromising than that of men? Among men, do not those who cease to do evil and seek to do good obtain grace?

No, not grace, for grace cannot be earned. If, therefore, you talk of 'grace', do not speak of *earning* it, unless by 'grace' you mean 'wages' or 'reward'. If that is what you mean, then stop calling it 'grace'. A gift is no longer a gift once you have paid for it, and it ceases to be a blessing once it becomes a reward.

4.
The meaning of the word 'grace'

My old friend had yet to learn the truths we have just seen in the previous chapter and had no idea of the misapprehension under which he laboured. When I asked him if he thought that the forgiveness of sins and eternal life were a free gift from God, he replied confidently: 'I am persuaded of that, and that is the basis of my faith. Certainly, salvation is by the grace of God, and I do not believe that anyone can be saved except through the one who died on this cross.'

Such inconsistency would have surprised me, coming as it did from a man whose speech and behaviour indicated an educated mind and great intelligence, had I not recognized in his words the same kind of reasoning that I had once held myself, and that I had so often met among Christians these days.

Indeed, if you ask the majority of those who profess to believe in the Lord Jesus, what is their hope for eternal salvation, almost all of them will reply that they expect to receive it by the mercy and grace of God through Jesus Christ. It is, they add, in order to obtain this and to make themselves worthy of it, at least as far as it is possible for man to do so, that they go to church, carry out all the requirements of their religion, give to the poor and refrain from any immoral conduct.

Thus, on the one hand, they use the expressions, 'the Saviour', 'grace', 'free forgiveness' and 'the gift of God', while, on the other, they strive to deserve and earn by their own efforts the forgiveness of their sins and the wonderful blessings which accompany it. In their folly they are just like the bankrupt debtor who boasted of having been released from all debt by the king in person, but still scrimped and saved because he was afraid that he might be imprisoned if he did not pay off the whole debt himself.

This was my companion's mistake. I wanted to tell him so, but I had first to show him the full extent of his error, so that the truth would then appear even more striking. This precaution proved necessary, I found, in such cases.

If you show a pupil a beautiful work of art and then help him to make his own copy of it before he has seen all that is wrong with his own technique, there is a risk that he will always regret the destruction of the poor copy which gave him such pleasure to draw and which to his eyes looked as good as the original.

I therefore asked the old man when he hoped to have this grace conferred on him. Did he think that the Lord Jesus would himself soon grant him forgiveness of his sins and entrance into paradise?

'Well, ... I don't know,' he replied in some embarrassment. 'In my youth, when I was in the army, I wasn't altogether blameless, I must admit. But, since settling down in a very happy marriage, I can say that I have lived an honest and upright life. Not, of course, that I have been any better than many of my peers, but at least I have never infringed the laws of honour or those of the land. If doing good to others is a good work, as well as one of the purest sources of pleasure, then perhaps I could mention that too.

'As for my religion, my position in society (I have a post in a neighbouring province) means that I have had to set an example, and I try to submit faithfully to all that our Holy Mother Church requires. Surely, then, I have a reasonable hope of being received in grace, haven't I?'

'You are very fortunate,' I replied, 'to have been able to escape from the hustle and bustle of the world and to have made yourself useful to others. I can see that your way of life has earned you the respect of those around you. But would it be indiscreet of me to ask whether you have done these things for God or for yourself?'

'For myself!' he answered, after a moment's thought. 'Well ... in some respects, at least. I admit that I have found happiness in a quiet, peaceful life with an excellent wife and surrounded by a family that was all I could wish for. But in enjoying these things, I don't think I have done anything other than what the good God who gave them to me intended.'

'I don't think so, either,' I replied. 'But what I am asking is if all the good that you have done, whether in the secrecy of your own heart and conscience, or out of kindness to your neighbour or duty to your religion, has been a demonstration of your love for God, or rather an expression of your desire to gain God's favour, the forgiveness of your sins and, in the end, the salvation of your soul?'

My question went straight to the conscience of this honest man. He weighed it up for a few moments, and then admitted: 'I see that if a man is guilty of self-seeking when he does good with an eye to receiving a reward from God, then I have fallen into that trap. I confess that what you have said has made a deep impression on me. But tell me this: aren't my intentions good if I am obeying God's commandments, not with a vulgar desire to show others what a good fellow I am, but in order to hear God say one day, "Well done, good and faithful servant"? (Matt. 25:21). Isn't that the very motive that God wants us to have?'

I replied, 'Suppose that I am a rebellious soldier, but I try to obey the king's commands, either because I am afraid that if my rebellion were discovered it would lead to my being put to death, or so that I might gain the king's favour. However much I might try to play down, or keep

22

quiet about, the reasons for my actions, it would still be true that I was seeking my own ends, and working only for my own security. My actions would be guided by the law of constraint, not by my own free will, and still less by love. If I stood up and started marching, it would be because I was driven to it on the one hand by the fear of punishment, and on the other hand by self-interest, in the hope of a reward.'

How difficult it is for the heart of man to understand this when it is a question of his own obedience to God's commandments! We quickly recognize for what they are the efforts of someone to gain his superior's goodwill, and we regard any show of submission or zeal on the part of the subordinate as mere self-interest. However, when it comes to the position of the sinner before God, immediately the very same motives are viewed differently and called by a different name. Then we say, and declare in our preaching, that the man who to some degree curbs the worst excesses of his behaviour out of fear of the Last Judgement, and the one who gives away to others some of his possessions which he does not really need, and is assiduous in carrying out his daily devotions or retreats into a life of penitent asceticism, in order to wipe out his previous misdeeds and to open the way to heaven — this man, we say, does all this 'for the love of God'! As if love can go hand in hand with fear! As if love can never become mercenary and only love in its own interest!

The old man evidently sensed that my reply carried with it this reproach, for he said to me very earnestly, 'If

I understand you aright, sir, you are telling me that if I have practised my religion in order to gain God's approval, and therefore the forgiveness of my sins, then I have done it all for myself and not for God... Now I come to look at it, I see that you are right. Yes, perhaps without my realizing it, even the least ostentatious of my acts have secretly been tainted with these wrong motives. This is very serious! I wonder if there is anyone at all who can be virtuous for any other motive than self-interest.'

'Don't you think,' I replied, 'that if the king was pleased to grant me a full and free pardon for all my misdemeanours, I would be certain of my immunity from the law? From that moment, the motives for my obedience would be totally different from those I had before I received the royal favour, wouldn't they?'

'But,' my companion was quick to respond, 'that's because you would be assured of your pardon. You would therefore be free to follow, without any need for anxious striving, the dictates of a heart full of gratitude!'

'Well, then,' I went on, with the same earnestness with which he had spoken, touching the cross with my hand, 'if a sinner believes that God has paid all his debts and granted him the gift of eternal life through the blood of the new covenant which was shed on this cross, will that sinner, thus vindicated, still do all he can to obtain that forgiveness? Will he not rather follow, without any anxious striving, the dictates of a heart that the certainty of this blessing has filled with gratitude?'

5.
Self-interest versus love

The old man appeared surprised, and I could see that this was a totally new idea to him. His reply showed that he was still trying to grasp the sense of what he had just heard. 'Certainly,' he said, 'if I believed that God had already forgiven my sins ... I would stop thinking that I must earn forgiveness...'

'And the motive for all your good works,' I continued, 'would no longer be fear of punishment or the desire to get to heaven.'

'No ... no doubt... Obviously,' he said, 'I cannot try to earn what has already been given to me by grace.'

'So, you see, if you consider salvation as a gift, as the grace of God, then you can no longer have any thought of trying to earn his forgiveness.'

'I admit, sir, that I had not thought about the word "grace" in that way before, and I can see that I was mistaken. For in the end, salvation is either a gift or a reward, a wage. If it is a gift, why should I try to earn it? But that was what I was doing, and I was wrong. However, this doesn't help me. I can see that it is absolutely necessary to live a good life in order to reach heaven. So I still come back to this point where I say, if I don't do the things that God commands me to do, then there will be no salvation for me. I must, therefore, carry out these good works in order to ... gain salvation.'

'You can at least see, can't you,' I replied, 'that if the law says to you, "Be sober, or else you will perish," and if grace says to you, "Be sober, because you have been redeemed," you will do the same thing in both cases, but from completely different motives?'

'Say rather that they are totally incompatible, not just different,' corrected the old man. 'The law will compel me through fear, whereas grace will influence me by love.'

'If, then, your sins are forgiven through grace, they cannot at the same time be forgiven through the law. That means that if this forgiveness of sins is carried out by means of a Saviour, and because of what he has done, it is totally futile, a contradiction in terms even, to try to gain it by obedience to the law.

'If the king, by an act of goodwill, tells me that he forgives me for my rebellion, how can I think of earning this free and sovereign pardon by some later act of submission? I must, therefore, sinful and worthy of punishment as I am, make a conscious choice between, on the one hand, a pardon that I will try to gain by my own obedience and, on the other, a totally different pardon that will be freely given to me.

'Now, if I choose one, then I renounce all claim to the other. How could we possibly try to reconcile them? One originates from me, a sinner living here on earth; the other comes down from God, who is holy and dwells in the unapproachable light of heaven.

'So if I say, "I will obey God's commandments in order to gain forgiveness," I am in fact saying that I consider this pardon as a wage or a reward. I will have earned it by my works, my practices, my religious observances, my groans and tears. If I receive it, it is because it is owed to me.

'But if, on the contrary, I speak of it in a totally different way, saying, "I recognize that I am justly condemned and unable to help myself in any way; I can look only to the goodness of God, to his mercy and pure grace, for the forgiveness of my sins," in so doing I declare that this pardon does not owe anything to me. There is no way in which I could earn it.'

'In other words, sir,' asked my companion, 'if I, who recognize that I am a sinner, do what I can to earn this forgiveness, then I am, by that very act, turning my back on the grace of God?'

'That is exactly what one of the apostles says when he writes, "If [salvation is] by grace, then it is no longer of works; otherwise, grace is no longer grace. But if it is of

27

works, it is no longer grace; otherwise work is no longer work" (Rom. 11:6).'

'What a new way of looking at this important subject!' exclaimed the old man. 'Put like that, it can only be one thing or the other. But how solemn it all is! For if salvation is by grace (and there's no doubt of that!), then what have I been doing all this time trying to seek it through works? For all these years, I have been building up all my devotions, almsgiving, prayers and religious observances — and all for nothing, nothing at all!'

'Judge for yourself, sir,' I replied. 'If you have done all these things in order to earn your forgiveness and to gain a place in heaven, then you have certainly turned your back on grace in looking only for a reward.'

6.
Grace leaves no room for pride

'I have been mistaken, then!' exclaimed the old man, with an expression of mingled surprise and grief. 'Yes, I was deceiving myself about my motives when I thought I was doing all these things out of love for God! Now I see that I did them all out of self-interest. What a dreadful discovery to make!'

After some thought I asked, 'Why do you say it's "dreadful" when the Lord is granting you a notable blessing? I ask you, which would you prefer? To continue under this dangerous misapprehension, or to see it and be freed from it?'

'That's true,' he replied, nodding his head. 'But I have lost the whole of my life!'

'And if the Son of God,' I rejoined, 'gives you his in its place, will you lose out by such an exchange?'

The old man looked at me for a few moments, and then said softly, 'Will you say that again, please?'

'I am asking you,' I repeated, 'if you would prefer to keep your own works, or cast them aside and receive those of the Lord Jesus in their place. For either your works or his must accompany your soul to the judgement seat of God. So do you want to be rich in your own resources, or to rely solely on the wealth of the Redeemer?'

How readily this choice would have been made if this man loved his God! How easy and pleasant it would be for the creature to acknowledge that he was nothing before his Creator, and to receive all from him, if that creature adored his Maker! How eagerly and gratefully the sinner would cast away all confidence in himself, and welcome, seize and embrace the grace and righteousness of his Lord, if the Lord was dearer to him than his own pride! How gladly we would receive this loving and glorious Saviour, who comes to us from the bosom of the Father, if the mercy and love of God surpassed in our eyes the attractiveness of the sins we commit or the glory we hope to achieve for ourselves!

But man prefers himself to God. The idea that the Lord should be the prime mover in the work of salvation is the very last thing he is prepared to concede.

Thus my elderly companion was fighting against the grace of God. Take heed, dear reader, that in your heart you do not make the same mistake and fail to give God the glory which is due to him.

'Does that mean,' asked my friend somewhat resentfully, 'that there is no difference between me and those scoundrels who care nothing for religion or morals? Doesn't God take any account of a person's integrity, or of a way of life which is at least ... honourable?'

'Either you are pure and blameless in his eyes,' I replied gravely, 'or you are a sinner in some respect...'

'But who isn't a sinner?' he broke in.

'Well then, who isn't under condemnation?' I answered firmly. 'Don't let us deceive ourselves here: either we have done *everything* that is right, and therefore are righteous and have no need of forgiveness; or we have done wrong, even if it is only in a few things, and are therefore guilty. We cannot, therefore, stand before God, except insofar as he purifies us.

'You must think about it for yourself, but speaking for myself, I confess to you, in the presence of God, that if God himself had not washed me and cleansed me from my sins, I would still at this very moment be under his wrath. So I declare openly that if I have received forgiveness, then it is not because of anything I have done. However upright and honourable I may have been in the sight of my fellow-men, the only grounds on which I can stand before God are that he has granted me exactly the same grace that he showed to the thief who hung on the cross by the side of the Redeemer.'

A long silence followed these words. The old man seemed agitated. He was debating the matter with himself, and I could see that the truth was struggling in his soul against misconceptions that he had held for a long

31

time, or rather against the unbelief which had given rise to and sustained them.

'So eternal life is a gift of grace!' he said finally with a sigh, and speaking more to himself than to me. 'It is a gift, and it comes to us purely and simply by the mercy of the Almighty! So if I receive it, then I must prostrate myself to the ground and confess that, far from having deserved it, I have only been granted it because I am unworthy of it!

'How man's pride is brought low, and how it is shown up as being deceitful and contemptible before the sovereignty of the Lord in bestowing mercy on us!

'It must be so,' he added, clasping his hands together. 'Salvation must come down in its entirety from the mercy-seat of God... There is no way it could originate from the guilty person and rise up to his judge! How mistaken I was! What darkness I was in!' he continued, looking at me. 'Oh, sir, what have I done with my common sense up till now? How could I have imagined and stubbornly convinced myself that I should purify my soul by my own efforts, and act in a way which detracts from the grace of God?

'I have wasted all my life! It has all been wasted!' he repeated over and over again, shaking his head and groaning. 'Alas, I have done even worse than that, for I have fled from God's mercy in trying to save myself.'

'But God has not fled far from you,' I replied gently. 'No, he has not rejected you. He has seen you lost in error and he has saved you from it, for today, at this very moment, he is revealing his truth to you. He is telling you that the forgiveness of sins, as well as the gift of eternal life, is to be found in him alone, that is, in the person of his holy Son, Jesus Christ, who did not die in vain when he shed his blood on this cross. It was not in vain that he suffered in his own soul the penalty due to condemned sinners.'

'I understand,' replied the man a little more calmly, 'and that, I think, is what I have never seen until now. Jesus took upon himself the curse from which he delivered men.'

'What did you think he did, then?' I asked.

'I always believed (because that is what we are taught)', he answered, 'that by his death on the cross the Son of God took away the curse which hangs over the whole of Adam's race by nature, and that in this way he opened up for us the means of obtaining a salvation to which we would never otherwise have had access.'

'That is what I too believed when I walked alone, far from the Word of God and following the teaching passed on to me by other men like me. I too thought, at that time, that the Lord had taken away all the obstacles which surrounded the mountain of salvation. It was then up to me to climb it and to drag myself up, as it were, by the bootstraps of my own works, until I reached the heights of forgiveness and glory.

'I did not know the meaning of the word "Saviour". I

treated him merely as an aid to salvation, at best of some use to someone who is already righteous in himself, but of no use at all to a creature who is "dead in trespasses and sins", as the Scripture says (Eph. 2:1).

'And so, sir, since I was convinced that my salvation was something I had to work for myself, I put a great deal of effort into achieving it. I did one good work after another; I kept a very careful watch on my natural inclinations; I spent more and more time in prayers and devotions; I gave alms and imposed penances on myself; I wore out my body by my fasting and denied myself any form of pleasure or relaxation. In this way I was piling up misshapen stones with no cement on the shifting sands of my own presumptuousness. At every new sin, my wall would crumble away. In my folly I tried yet again to build it up and to bind it together by ever more tears and more solemn vows.

'God himself revealed my mistake to me. He did it, as he always does, through his Word. I began to read the Holy Bible, first of all very warily and with all kinds of prejudices (for you know how little we are taught to read it). Then my attention and interest were caught. So it was that, by degrees, I came to see the truth that man by himself is lost, and that the whole of salvation, from beginning to end, is the free gift of God in Jesus Christ.

'I believed this truth, or, rather, by his Holy Spirit God enabled me both to understand and believe it. Now I have peace in my soul, for I am convinced, according to what

34

God himself has testified in his Word, that my sins have been freely forgiven. I know that everywhere and at all times I have free access to the throne of grace and that the one who sits upon that throne is my Father, and no longer my Judge.

'I therefore come before him boldly, for I am led by my Advocate. He is this same High Priest who, on the cross, cleansed my soul in his own blood. This is what I now believe, and this is the peace which I now enjoy' (Heb. 10:19-23).

'I would give anything, sir,' replied the old man feelingly, 'to know that peace too! Please be patient with me and tell me how you came to obtain this tremendous blessing.'

7.
A personal testimony

'I discovered this peace,' I replied, 'on the very day that I understood and believed what God tells us about the sacrifice of his Son on the cross. I had often read and heard these words, and I had repeated them hundreds of times, but I had never given them their proper meaning, nor understood the force of them.

'One day, when I was reading the Epistle to the Hebrews, I was very much struck by the passages where it says that the Son of God had by himself purged the sins of his people and by this sacrifice had made perfect for ever those whom the Father has given him (Heb. 1:3; 2:17; 10:10-14, etc.). I thought a lot about this and came to the conclusion that to try to do something to accomplish this salvation totally contradicts the fact that the Son of God has saved his people, as these passages teach.

'This first idea, which made good sense to me and restored to Jesus his true rôle, that of a perfect Saviour, was quickly followed by another which troubled me greatly. Since Jesus has saved for ever those for whom he offered himself as a sacrifice, it is clear that he did not offer himself for those who will be lost. For if he had offered himself on their behalf, they would have been cleansed from their sins, including those of unbelief and stubbornness, and would not therefore be dead in their sins. I then wondered anxiously: "Am I, or am I not, one of those sinners whom the Son of God has made perfect by the shedding of his blood?"'

'I beg you to tell me,' interrupted the old man excitedly, 'when and how you came to know the answer.'

'Well, I found it very difficult to be sure about it, and I didn't accept it without a struggle.'

'Whatever do you mean? Surely you don't have to be forced to learn something like that and to be assured of it?'

'This truth overturns our pride and tramples it into the dust. Mine did not submit easily. But in the end God was the stronger, and his truth set me free.'

'Well, then,' he insisted, 'how did God do it?'

'By graciously enabling me to imitate the faith of Abraham (Gal. 3), that is, to believe purely and simply in the Word of God, and to put my trust in what it proclaims and promises. Let me explain.

'From the moment when I first understood that the Lord Jesus has saved for ever those for whom he gave himself on the cross, I also came to the conclusion, as I

37

have said, that I needed to be sure that I was one of those sinners. But here I made a great mistake. I thought that, in order to be sure of this, I needed to be able to find in myself the obedience and holiness which characterize the Saviour's true disciples.'

'But,' prompted my companion, 'weren't you right to think that? If I don't have the characteristics of a believer, I surely can't persuade myself that I am one, can I?'

'No, of course not. But we need to realize that, as these visible characteristics (such as love, joy, peace, a patient spirit, and all the other outworkings of holiness) are the fruits of the Holy Spirit, I must have received the Holy Spirit *before* I can even begin to produce any of these fruits.

'Now, since the Holy Spirit is given, like an anointing of joy and holiness, only *after* a person has believed God's Word, it was clear that I had first to believe the Lord's promise. All the time I had not believed, I was wrong to look for evidences of holiness in myself which could not possibly appear until *after* I had believed the promise.'

'I'm afraid I must seem very ignorant,' said my companion, 'but I must confess that I don't really understand the distinction.'

'You know, since you believe the Bible, that God gave his church several commandments which they must keep.'

'Didn't God give his laws to all men?' he asked.

'What is contained in the law of God is mandatory on all who hear it. The one who hears it but does not put it into practice is regarded as a sinner. But the things which the Father of the family asks of his children by the mouth of their elder Brother are addressed to the family alone.

'In the same way that it is a great mistake to impose on a stranger the duties required of a son, you must not expect from someone who is still in unbelief the obedience that is only possible when the heart is enabled by faith. An unbeliever is guided by the spirit of the world alone, but the believer is guided by the Spirit of God. How can you, then, expect the same result from two such opposing sources? How can you say to someone who fears condemnation and the wrath of God, "Behave like one of God's beloved children"?'

'Yes, I see, that is the distinction which I had failed to make,' the old man admitted. 'Now I understand. If God's commandments are given to the human race in general as a law which imposes obligations and constraints on them, for God's children, the family of the redeemed, this same law comes as the instructions of a loving Father.'

'Nothing is clearer,' I assured him. 'It is the Spirit of Christ who enables us to understand, love and follow his commands. He must therefore be present in someone *before* that person can understand, love and follow the Father's commands. But this Spirit, whom the world (that is, mankind in general) does not possess, is given as a seal only to believers. I must, therefore, believe *before* I can understand, love and follow my Father's commands.

'I will only be tormenting myself in vain if I insist on finding and producing in myself a love of God's law and the submission of my will to that of the Lord *before* I have received, by faith, the assurance that God has made me his child and is therefore my loving Father through Jesus' (Eph. 1:13; Gal. 5:22-23).

'I understand everything you have been saying, sir,' exclaimed my elderly companion, 'and I can see what you were doing to assure yourself that you belonged to Jesus. You wanted to find obedience in yourself, and to conclude from that that you were among the redeemed, didn't you?'

'Exactly. I plagued myself with worry about this for a long time. But at last God brought me through, as I have said, by leading me to believe as Abraham believed: in other words, to believe not only without finding any evidence of holiness in myself, but actually in spite of all the evidence to the contrary that I found there.

'I had read, one day, the story of the royal official who, having urged the Lord Jesus to come and heal his son, believed the Saviour's words when he told him, "Go, your son lives" (John 4:46-53). The thought then came to me that this man had no proof, no tangible evidence of the truth of what had been stated. He had only the word of the Lord Jesus, the statement that he made. Nevertheless, as soon as he had heard that word, the official went away, and stopped asking the Lord to come and see his child. His assurance of deliverance was therefore based entirely on Jesus' words. He relied on them in complete confidence. "The Lord has said it; therefore it is true." That was this man's reasoning.

'This example then led me to that of Abraham, who believed God in spite of all the evidence, in himself and in Sarah, which was contrary to what God had promised. Abraham never doubted that what God had told him would come to pass, even if it seemed impossible to human eyes (Rom. 4:18-25; Gal. 3). "It is the faith of this believer," I said to myself, "which is set before us as an example! I must, therefore, do as he did: I must believe God, purely and simply, and believe all that he promises. If God declares that whoever believes in him is justified, then I must be assured that this applies to me and that if I believe, then I am justified.

'Thereupon, I wondered how both the royal official and Abraham came to have assurance that they truly believed. I saw that neither of these believers had any other proof that he was a believer than the belief itself which was in his heart.

'I therefore examined myself very carefully, according to the command of the apostle Paul (2 Cor. 13:5), and I sought to discover what I truly believed concerning the Lord Jesus. I recognized that I believed in him, because I knew him in my soul and believed all that God has said and testified concerning his Son. I could, therefore, say

41

to God in my heart, "I believe that you so loved the world that you sent your only begotten Son into the world. Yes, I believe and am assured that Jesus came from you and that you sent him. I also believe with all my heart that it is in him, and in him alone, that you have given us eternal life. I am sure that I worship Jesus Christ, even though I have never seen him or heard his voice'" (John 3:15-18; 17:8; 1 John 5:11; 1 Peter 1:8).

'But how did that belief give you peace in your soul?' asked the old man.

8.

The Saviour's work is complete

I answered the old man's question by saying, 'God enabled me also to believe the promise that is given to all those who truly believe in Jesus: that is, that "Whoever believes in the name of the Son of God may know that he has eternal life" (John 1:12; 3:36; 6:47; 11:26-27; 20:31; 1 John 5:13).

'Since I had the happiness of believing in the name of the Son of God, I was then able to conclude that I had eternal life, according to the promise of God. From that day on I have had peace in my heart, and I have devoted myself to obeying God in the way that he requires of his children, for he says he has made me one of them.'

'I am beside myself, sir, listening to you,' he said, 'for everything you say is so simple and so powerful, yet so opposed to everything that, until today, I thought was right. It seems to have made nonsense of every word of my religion.'

'I am not at all surprised. I can easily imagine from my own experience the misconceptions you have been under, and I don't hesitate to say that, until now, you have seen Jesus merely as a helper, even if you have called him "Saviour".'

'No, you've got it wrong. I have never thought or said anything different from what I say again now, before this holy cross — that Jesus Christ is the Saviour, and there is no other.'

'Amen! May his name be blessed for ever! But the fact that you confess it with your lips means very little if your mind does not comprehend it and, most of all, if your heart does not believe it.'

'But I assure you, my dear sir,' cried my companion indignantly, 'that I do believe it with all my heart! Here, before the Lord, the Creator of the heavens and the earth, I confess the name of the Father, the Son and the Holy Spirit. I affirm, in particular, that I believe in Jesus, the Son of God and the Saviour of the world.'

'Very well, then. What meaning do you give the word "Saviour", seeing that your belief in Jesus as Saviour has not stopped you from trying to save yourself? The surety given for a debtor is totally inadequate, to my mind, if it leaves him still fearing imprisonment.'

'But ... I believe that Jesus is the Saviour ... and that he has saved our souls by his death on the cross, provided that we, on our part, do all that he commands us in his Word and through the church.'

'My dear sir, do you realize what you are saying? The Saviour, you say, has saved us by his death, "provided that we do everything that he commands"! That means that, according to you, he has saved those who will, however, only be saved when they have fulfilled certain conditions. But is such a thing possible? Suppose, for example, that my debt was paid off this morning by a benefactor; would it only be discharged tomorrow, or the day after, when I had rendered this friend some service or other in expression of my gratitude?'

The old man was very much struck by this and he smiled and said, 'Oh well, that's another mistake on my part. You can see how ignorant I have been.'

I replied gravely, 'We are talking about a very serious and dangerous mistake if it deprives the Lord Jesus of his rôle as Saviour, and if it brings him down to the level of a helper who cannot be of any assistance to men without their goodwill! Your ignorance is fatal if it makes the gift of God of no effect and reduces it to the level of a mere offer which is rendered useless by the first refusal!'

'I beg your pardon! What do you mean? When and how have I ever rejected the Saviour or belittled his worth?'

'Sir, I am not judging or accusing you; I am only saying that there is no more fatal mistake than to see the Son of God merely as a kind of secondary deliverer, whose work has to be supplemented by moral actions or sacrifices on our part. And that, undoubtedly, is the mistake that you have just put into words.'

'I beg you to show me where I have gone wrong,' asked the old man, 'for if I have done so, it is, I repeat, purely through ignorance.'

'God states two things about salvation: firstly, that it is a *gift,* and secondly, that this gift is *in his Son* (1 John 5:11). This gift comprises both redemption from eternal condemnation and the possession of everlasting life. Jesus embodies in himself these two priceless gifts, for forgiveness of sins and the true, heavenly life are both to be found in him. So it is in Jesus that redemption from sins has been accomplished, just as it is in him that life, happiness and glory are to be found.

'That means that Jesus did not leave his work unfinished. He has not just half saved us, but he has perfected and brought to completion the salvation that he was sent to accomplish.

'So we see that Holy Scripture calls him a "propitiation" and "the Lamb of God who takes away sin". It also states that "He himself purged the sins of his people." By his sacrifice on the cross, he has made perfect for ever those who are being sanctified and those whom the Father has given him (Rom. 3:25; 1 John 2:2; John 1:29; Heb. 1:3; 2:17; 10:10-14; John 17:2; Isa. 53:8, etc.).

'It is for this reason that the church can declare that Jesus "has redeemed us from the curse of the law, having become a curse for us" on the cross. He was wounded and bruised for the iniquities that were laid on him. He was stricken for the transgression of his people. It is thus that the church has been cleansed and washed, so that she is holy and without blemish (Gal. 3:13; Isa. 53:1-6,8; Eph. 5:23-27).

'Thus speaks the church. Whether we turn to the prophets, the epistles or the book of Revelation, the Word of God reveals this great truth, that the Lord Jesus has in himself fully accomplished the salvation of his beloved sheep, whose sins he bore in his own body on a shameful gibbet like this one. He has delivered them for ever from the condemnation that they should otherwise have had to undergo themselves.'

'If you are right,' said my companion, 'then once again I admit that until now I have had completely the wrong idea about the work of the Saviour, for I certainly never understood that the salvation of the church has been accomplished and completed by the death of the Son of God.'

'What exactly did you think, then?'

'As I have already told you,' he explained, 'I have always believed that the Saviour, by his sacrifice, took away from our souls our original sin, and opened the way to salvation. By that I mean that by his death he removed the barrier of condemnation which prevented mankind from being able to approach God. In this way, I thought, he opened the way for us to perform works by which we can earn salvation.'

'Oh, sir, your thinking on the gift of God in Jesus Christ was so narrow! How little this salvation, this grace of God, would be worth, if all it achieved was to allow man to save himself! You have credited God's love towards his people with so little power! How cheaply you have regarded the blood shed upon the cross by the only begotten Son of God! Don't you see? According to you, the effectiveness of the Saviour's work is limited to a kind of help or aid, which the scorn and the pride of the sinner can render totally ineffective.

'Oh, what a pathetic Saviour you imagined him to be! Or rather, what a caricature of salvation you have made of the sacrifice of the Lamb! With what contempt you have treated his agony and death! Wasn't I right when I said that you spoke of the Son of God merely as a kind of secondary deliverer, who depended on the goodwill of men before he can bring about or, rather, make easier, a salvation which man has to accomplish for himself?'

9.
The old man sees the truth at last

My companion remained silent. He was turning over in his mind all that I had just said, and what he had heard was having an effect on him.

'Such love!' he exclaimed, in a voice full of adoration. 'God has shown such love! What a salvation! What an amazing, wonderful redemption!... Oh, I see it now! I have never understood the Saviour's sacrifice until now. Oh, I was so far from seeing what it meant! Alas! How ignorant and hard-hearted I have been!'

'Yes,' I continued, 'our minds are so limited when it comes to reflecting on such great mercy! If the king had stepped down from his throne for us and had given his own life on the scaffold to save ours, we would understand and extol such wonderful clemency. We would take delight in praising it, and we would never dream of bringing it down to the level of a conditional pardon, or an attempt to meet us halfway which would only be effective if we followed it up by earning it.

'But when it comes to God, and the love which he has shown to us in Jesus, and to the Saviour's atoning sacrifice and the gift of eternal life which he himself has granted us — then, suddenly, our understanding is darkened and we no longer want to see the truth. Our minds and hearts vie with one another in striving to deny God the right to show mercy, and in minimizing, detracting from and if possible completely nullifying both the grace of the Lord and the gift which it entails!'

'So,' interrupted my friend, 'if I have understood you rightly, you say that when Jesus offered himself on the cross, he underwent in his own soul all the condemnation that his church would otherwise have suffered herself if she had not been saved?'

'That, sir, is the truth. It is also what distinguishes grace from all the thousands of false religions which serve only to deceive men and lead them astray. The children of God, taught as they are by the Word and the Spirit of God, see in Jesus a Saviour, and not merely a helper. They therefore believe that the Father has given his only begotten Son to redeem his church completely and for all eternity.

'In order to carry out his Father's will, the Son has, by a great mystery, united himself to this church. He bore the punishment that she deserved, and he gave her life in himself by the almighty power of the Holy Spirit.

'True faith believes, then, that Jesus is indeed a Saviour. False faith, on the other hand, rejects this truth.

It wants to see the sacrifice of the Son of God merely in terms of someone being martyred for his views, or a conditional offering to which sinners must add their own sacrifices, or at the very least, their good intentions, before it will have the power needed to save them.'

'Now I understand,' he said. 'Yes, I understand what the cross of Jesus was, and what a sacrifice he offered there. Jesus is one with his church; he bore her sins in his soul, and he saved her — yes, he saved her effectively, by suffering the condemnation that she deserved... Oh, what a new light this sheds on Jesus and the shedding of his blood!'

'Do you believe now? Do you see that God does not save by halves, and that this salvation isn't a half measure made available to man, for him to complete?'

'No, definitely not!' replied the old man with great emotion. 'The Lord is no less gracious than an earthly king. When the king grants a free pardon, he doesn't expect the guilty person to carry on pleading his cause, nor does he keep him in fear of the scaffold.'

'That is why, sir,' I continued solemnly, 'you ought to have believed what God was saying to you about this grace, and not keep setting up your own works, your almsgiving and religious observances, in opposition to it.'

10.
Man's pride insults the Saviour

My words of reproach did not fall on deaf ears. The old man remained silent. His eyes were lowered and he appeared to be deep in thought. I left him to his reflections. Several minutes passed before he said quietly, 'So I was denying the cross even while I was worshipping it! I was rejecting the Saviour and his grace by the very things that I was doing to win them for myself! I was groping around in such darkness and I caused myself so much anxiety!... And all that, I now realize, because of my pride — yes, because of my self-esteem, and in the hope of acquiring some merit in God's eyes... Oh! I am amazed at how foolish I have been!'

'You were certainly in error in trying to complete something that you thought the Lord had merely begun, and in trying to add something to the sacrifice of the Son of God. It is also a very strange contradiction in terms to call Jesus "Saviour" and yet at the same time make every effort to deny him this rôle by working at earning your own salvation — in other words, trying to save yourself.'

'So, in order to find rest,' he exclaimed in wonderment, 'my soul must look to this sacrifice made on the cross, and to that alone!... I must cast myself on the Saviour's mercy and I must lay down at his feet the weapons of my pride and my worthless pretensions! How new it all is to me! I will have to completely lay aside all my good works and all my religious observances!'

'Yes, grace demands that we divest ourselves of everything and totally renounce all our errors. Here the bankrupt soul files its petition and admits to its ruin before it can look for the surety. The Saviour has come to seek and to save what is *already lost*. It is not a matter of something which has just gone astray or is in danger of getting lost. Now, the man who tries to meet Jesus halfway, showing him his good intentions and the sacrifices he has made, and saying, "You cannot refuse me your heaven, for here is enough to pay for it, more or less" — that man does not think he is lost.'

'Then all that effort was for nothing!' groaned my companion. 'What a terrible thing to find out!... For you would be amazed, I am sure, if I told you all the things I have done, or wanted to do, in order to gain forgiveness — this forgiveness that God gives freely in his holy Son, Jesus. What a fool I was to wear myself out in privations, hardships and any number of ceremonies and religious observances and to want to substitute all these things for the love of Jesus, and to rely on all my vain illusions instead of the blood that he shed on the cross!... Oh, how much secret unbelief there was in all these devotions, and how my piety was really dishonouring to God!'

'Certainly,' I agreed, 'if the king saves the life of a criminal by putting his own son to death on the scaffold, it would be the height of unbelief, or even madness, for the criminal who has been saved by such an act of grace to start fasting and weeping in the hope of obtaining his pardon.'

'Yet how many thousands of Christians make this very mistake! To tell you the truth, the danger that they are in frightens me. And, alas! the more they go in for their devotions and the more Pharisaical they become, the greater the peril they are in. There is such widespread ignorance about salvation! All those souls who, in order to save themselves — yes, save *themselves* — surround themselves with precautions and barriers, and burden themselves to breaking-point with readings, prayers, religious observances and rituals are really pouring scorn on the work and sacrifice of the Redeemer. They know nothing at all of the grace of God and the perfect love of his Son!'

'We could go even further and say they are proudly resisting the Holy Spirit. Indeed, man's unbelief has grieved him in this way right down through the ages. The people of Israel resisted him in the desert by their idolatry. Then again in the promised land they resisted him when they refused to listen to the prophets. The most devout zealots of the nation opposed him yet again when the Son himself, sent from the very bosom of the Father, told them that eternal life is a gift, which no human effort can even begin to earn.

'The same thing is happening today. Jesus is proclaimed, preached and depicted as being crucified, as it were, before men's very eyes. He is portrayed as what he truly is, as the Saviour, in whom is to be found salvation in all its fulness. His messengers are sent throughout the world to proclaim clearly: "The blood of the Son of God is the only ransom acceptable to God for souls which are captives of unrighteousness; this blood has been shed for the remission of the sins of many, and, by rising from the dead, Jesus has obtained for ever the salvation of his people."

'This proclamation is published, written and displayed everywhere, time and time again; symbols and monuments remind us of it; a cross like this one is a constant witness to it; people hear it, they listen and pretend to believe it ... but at the same time they make a mockery of it and make it of no effect by preparing and carrying out works which are supposed to take the place of the Saviour's sacrifice, or at least to make up for what it lacks!

'So in this way so-called "Christian" churches, families — whole nations even — grieve the Spirit of truth by despising his testimony. They bring down on themselves the terrible judgement that God pronounces on unbelievers, which consists of abandoning them to the hardness of their hearts and leaving them enmeshed in the twisted and tangled net of their vain doctrines, which, the Lord says, are only the commandments of men.'

11.
Taking God at his word

As I continued to testify to all the fulness of what was involved in the sacrifice of the Lord Jesus, and to the free gift of salvation accomplished by the Father in his beloved Son, the old man listened all the more attentively and his expression bore witness to the joy afforded him by the contemplation of such great lovingkindness. It was easy to trace the progress made in his thinking by the truth of salvation by grace and to see how it was beginning to dispel his errors and doubts.

Nevertheless, I wanted to know if this truth, in which alone there is life, had penetrated to his heart, or if he had only grasped it intellectually. I therefore spoke to him of his great age, of the uncertainty of life and the solemn entrance of the soul into eternity, and I asked him if he would joyfully welcome the summons to leave this world whenever it should come.

'Oh! sir,' he replied, somewhat sadly, 'although an old man ought to have had his fill of living, he still surrounds himself with illusions. He doesn't relinquish without a struggle a lifetime's habit of seeing the light, of living and breathing. This resistance will only be overcome by a greatly superior force. The hand which loosens such bonds certainly needs to be much more powerful than mere resignation or philosophy.

'However,' he went on, with bent head and in a voice that betrayed his emotion, 'I hope that I am no longer a total stranger to such a force, and that the heavenly and invincible Guide has already taken me by the hand and begun my deliverance.'

So, as you see, dear reader, there were still doubts in his mind. If he had begun to understand and contemplate the gift of salvation, he had not yet fully grasped it and made it his own. For this is not the way faith expresses itself. Faith believes what God has said and declares that it is resting on his promise. It also rejoices when the message is one of peace.

If a poor man receives letters patent of nobility and has to leave his cottage for the palace of a king he loves, he does not bemoan having to leave behind his humble and wretched abode because he has become so used to living in the old shack. Nor is it in an attitude of doubt and uncertainty that he assumes the dignity with which he is being invested. He does not entertain any doubts about the kind welcome he will receive from the monarch. He has received his letters patent; he believes them and, on this evidence, he gladly leaves behind his poor patch of ground and takes off his homespun. He hurries confidently towards the new home where he will be able to rest from his labours and where wealth and honours will be lavished on him.

Such is the assurance of a man who relies on the word of another man. Why, then, should my elderly friend manifest such sadness and uncertainty in the face of the testimony of God himself, unless it was that he had not yet come to lean in his heart, in simple, honest faith, on that word? Evidently he had not yet taken hold of the promise of the King of kings and made it his own!

So I reproached him in these words: 'O man of little faith! Why do you still doubt? What are you waiting for before you lift up your soul and rejoice in the imminent expectation of seeing your God?'

'But,' he replied in some confusion, 'please tell me, how am I lacking in faith? Have I not confessed, according to my belief, that Jesus Christ is the Saviour? Yes, he is this perfect Saviour who has redeemed for ever those for whom he died on the cross. So what do you mean by saying I am still in unbelief?'

'I mean that you doubt,' I replied, affectionately but firmly, 'the truth of God's declaration that whoever believes in Jesus is saved, that God justifies him and forgives all his sins, and that he has eternal life.'

'I don't doubt that at all,' he answered in a tone that

brooked no argument. 'I assure you that I believe it every bit as sincerely as I believe in the very existence of Jesus.'

'Well, then,' I said, emphasizing each word, 'since God says to you, to you who believe in the name of his Son, that you are justified and have life, why do you respond by saying that you *hope* it is true? If God states it is so, are you right to say, "It is possible"?'

'But, my dear sir,' answered my friend, 'is that what God actually says? Does he really say that whoever has faith in Jesus is counted as righteous before God?'

'Certainly,' I replied, 'for that is the testimony that God has given about his Son. He declares, as we have seen, that this unique and perfect Saviour has redeemed — not *will redeem*, but *has redeemed* — for ever the sinners for whom he offered himself up on the cross.

'He also declares, by the same token, that whoever believes in Jesus is justified and will never see condemnation. If, then, a man can be sure, on examining himself, that he renounces all idea of justifying himself by his own virtues and that he trusts in Jesus Christ and in his finished work on the cross...'

'God is my witness,' interrupted the old man, clasping his hands in front of him, 'that I now acknowledge my error. I no longer have any thoughts of earning salvation, and I believe sincerely in the sacrifice and the perfect merits of the Saviour who was nailed to the wood which this cross represents, and who rose again...'

'And God, who is also my witness,' I continued joyfully, 'therefore says and declares that everyone who believes in this way in the name of the Lord Jesus must know that he is justified by this same faith, and that he has eternal life.'

12.
The old man admits his unbelief

'So what have I been doing here on earth for these past seventy-six years,' exclaimed my companion, with great feeling and conviction, 'seeing that I knew nothing of this love of God towards me? For though I have only just learned of it today, he showed his love to me on this cross when he took my debt on himself and paid it with his own blood.

'I was therefore loved by him and my ransom was already paid even at the time when I lived like a fool, following the evil ways of the world, and when I cared nothing for God or his holy Son!... Yes, even then I was the object of his grace. More than that, it was already mine in his heart and will, even when I was wearing myself out under the burden of all my useless works!... Oh, sir! What a day this is for my soul! I shall always bless the time that I met you at the foot of this cross!'

'Any praise that is due belongs to our loving heavenly Father alone, who planned our meeting and this pleasant time of relaxation together!' I protested. 'It is his grace which guided our conversation to the topic of his ever-lasting love in Jesus. It is his Spirit who has granted to me, a poor, weak disciple of the Saviour, the privilege of bearing witness to his sacrifice on the cross, and has enabled you, whom he has been calling for so long, to hear and receive the truth. I am sure that you must have heard this truth many times, but your hearing was dulled by ignorance and unbelief, and...'

'Yes, by unbelief, my dear sir,' my friend interrupted. 'Now I am no longer under any illusions. I can clearly see that it was pride and hardness of heart that caused me to turn away until today from God's grace in Jesus. I refused to humble myself and I wanted to play some part in obtaining this great forgiveness. That was the root of my trouble; and I confess it in the presence of this mighty Saviour whom I now worship from the depths of my being as my Redeemer and my God. Yes, I believe it, for he says it: Jesus is my Saviour.'

'Your *Saviour*?' I repeated, alluding to the meaning that he had previously given to this beautiful word.

'Yes, my Saviour,' he replied, understanding, 'and no longer my helper. No, I no longer only half believe in the Son of God. I believe truly, with all my heart, and it is because I also believe his promise that my soul rests in peace at the foot of the cross.'

'Which cross do you mean?' I then asked. 'Do you mean these pieces of wood that I am touching now, or the actual offering and sacrifice of the Son of God?'

13.

The true cross cannot be touched

'This cross here,' said the old man, standing up and putting his hand on the wood, 'I now see as nothing more than a memorial. If it has been an idol, it is that no longer. No, never. The Lord Jesus himself has just taken away that error, that lie that I had cherished in my heart.

'My faith no longer looks towards this symbol that is being eaten away by worms. It looks to Jesus — to Jesus, the perfect Saviour whom the Father has given us, and who redeemed his church by dying on a cross, a gibbet like this one. It is his blood that I receive in my heart by faith in his holy name.'

'That is why,' I continued, also standing up, 'you must seize hold, freely and without fear, of this grace that the Father has granted us through his beloved Son in all its fulness. Do not look back, I beg you, to your old ways and practices. In Christ, God says, his children are made perfect; so what would you want with ceremonies and religious observances? Do you still want to use them to blot out your sins?'

'No, no!' said the old man, striking the ground with his stick. 'I have finished with such unbelief. No longer will I dishonour the Saviour's sacrifice by trying, even in the smallest degree, to substitute my works or prayers for what he has done. I have followed the dictates of my pride for far too long; it is time for me to bow to the leading of my God.'

14.
The need to study God's Word

'Take hold of the Word, then, my dear sir,' I urged him, 'and feed on it. Take my word for it, as a poor sinner who, after having wandered, like you, for many years in unbelief, found light, strength and comfort in God's book. Come to this treasure for yourself and draw from it all the riches of heaven that it contains.

'Make no mistake about it, the Lord did not cause his holy Word to be written down and translated into every language merely for man to hide it away or keep it sealed up. So think what it would mean if, just because during your days of error you kept it at a distance, you continued to put off reading it, delving into it and drinking from the living, pure and unquenchable source of peace and holiness? Wouldn't you be guilty once more of scorning the mercy of the Almighty and resisting the Holy Spirit, who dictated the Bible and who has just opened it up before you, saying, "Believe it and make it your own"?'

'I thank you for your concern,' replied my friend, squeezing my hand affectionately, 'and I accept your exhortation as coming from God himself. Yes, I have never appreciated the worth of God's Word, and I have replaced it, in my actions and my thoughts, with books and teachings that have blinded me to it and even drawn me further away from it. So I never understood God's love, or the fact that his grace was for me, and my way has been lit only by false glimmers of light that have led me astray. From now on, I will read and study this Word that contains both the title deed to my eternal inheritance and the commands of my Saviour and my Father. I assure you that I will take great delight in opening this treasure and searching through it.'

'May the Spirit of God enrich you with all the wealth that it contains!' I added prayerfully. 'For it is he alone who prepares our hearts to receive this true light and be guided by it. May he therefore himself be your sovereign Teacher and Guide as you study. He can never deceive you or lead you astray. So be upright in heart and faithful. Do not be afraid to hear and believe all that God will reveal to you, and do not hesitate to follow the path that his Word will make plain to you. For in the end, my dear sir, it will be far better for your soul to have listened to the Lord than to have been the disciple of men. The Word of the Lord will map out for you a route that is far safer than the one in which you walked when you followed the traditions of other sinners as weak and wavering as yourself.'

'I can see that already. I have in my soul even now the unshakeable proof of the authority of the Word of God over and above the most deeply rooted opinions, customs and practices. Could I possibly regard what has just happened to me, and which I can no longer deny even to myself, as being of very little importance? Isn't it God himself who has done this, by his all-powerful truth? Isn't it his Word that has humbled me before the Lord Jesus and, by making me despise all that I used to regard as giving me a right to salvation, has enabled me to find peace in a promise which I had previously thought to be very weak and certainly not enough by itself?'

'Just think what it will be like, then,' I went on, 'when the Spirit of the Lord, in the course of leading you into all this truth, has freed you more and more from the yoke and the bonds which held you captive, far from grace and, therefore, far from any true liberty. Then you will know what it means to advance towards death and eternity, not following after fables and uncertain theories, but treading firmly along a path where you can see the footprints of your Redeemer and your King.'

'Oh, may he speak to me and teach me, then! My soul can desire nothing else than to stay close to the one who will soon deliver it from this weak and decrepit body! For, after all, as you see, dear sir, I am already bent very low towards the ground which contains the dust of my ancestors.'

'Before we part, then, probably for ever here on earth, tell me once more,' I said, in a respectful but cordial manner, 'what your assurance is before God, and what you firmly expect from him when he summons you to pass into eternity.'

15.

The old man's confession of faith

'It is easy for me now,' replied the old man, with a contented smile, 'to make a confession of what I believe in all sincerity. Hear it, then, from my own lips, in the presence of our gracious God: "If the Lord God had not given a Saviour to the world, my soul would rightly have suffered condemnation. There was nothing at all it could do to avoid this condemnation. But, because God so loved the world that he gave his only begotten Son, that whoever believes in him should not perish but have everlasting life, and as I am sure in my heart that I believe in this holy Son of God, I am therefore also sure that I will not perish, but will possess everlasting life, for God himself tells me so.'

At that, this dear, venerable old man took me in his trembling arms and embraced me, saying with great tenderness, 'I clasp you to my heart because you are my brother in Christ and also my friend and benefactor. For it is you who today, through the Word of our God and by the power of his Holy Spirit, have turned me away from the lifeless, material cross that I used to worship and have led me to the true cross of the Son of God.'

Letter to a friend

'The truth will set you free' (John 8:32).

Letter to a friend

My dear friend,

I hear that you are ill, and even that you may be in danger of death, so I want to spend a few moments with you to bring you some words of peace, encouragement and true comfort.

Knowing, as I do, of your faith in the name of the Son of God, but also being aware that you entertain in your soul doubts concerning your own salvation, I want to speak to you about the need for you to take God at his word and to rest sincerely on the promise that he has made to us in Jesus, and on that alone.

The comfort of God's promise

How glad I am that I can approach you in the name of a Saviour and with the free promise of a life which, in all its entirety, is a gift of God's love to miserable, helpless sinners with no resources of their own!

It is so good to be able to greet a sick person, a mortal man on the point of passing into eternity, with a message of peace and pardon from the Lord and with God's own declaration that 'He who believes in the Son has everlasting life,' and 'He who believes in [Christ], though he may die, he shall live.'

These words will do your heart so much good at a time when your entrance into the invisible world and the presence of the Holy of Holies appears to be so close at hand and could even now fill you with alarm. How much you want to hear them as coming to you from the lips of God himself, and to have them made real to you in your own experience by the Spirit of adoption who is in Jesus! May he, therefore, be pleased to bless them to you and cause you to experience them in all their power!

Otherwise, how could our souls fail to be terrified at the very thought, not to mention the sight, of the judgement of God, carried out according to truth and justice? For sentence will be pronounced on the basis of the holy and unchangeable law that we have transgressed!

How could we bear even the very idea of appearing before the mighty God, the Holy One, with no possibility of taking refuge in self-deceit, pride or indifference? How could we endure hearing recounted everything we have done, especially those things known only to ourselves and of which our own consciences have so often reminded us during our life on earth, but which will then be seen for what they are in the full blaze of the light of truth, if we had no other refuge than our own tears, regrets and despair? All our innermost being shudders at the mere thought of such a thing, for 'God shows no partiality' and ' The soul who sins shall die.'

But as soon as the poor heart, convicted and weighed down by sin, hears the name of the Lord Jesus and these lovely words, 'Saviour, grace, remission of sins,' and 'everlasting life by faith in his blood', then it breathes again with hope. Its fears are relieved and it dares to look towards heaven, whence it hears this proclamation: 'God so loved the world [not just one nation], that he gave his only begotten Son, that whoever believes in him [in Jesus, the Son of God] should not perish but have everlasting life.' What wonderful news! What a gracious statement by the Lord himself! What welcome words for a poor, miserable sinner, condemned by his own conscience, who is searching for peace!

This peace is yours, my dear friend. Let death come, when God gives the order for it; it will be gladly welcomed as the messenger that will usher you into the presence of the one in whom you have life.

'But do I really have it?' you may ask, assailed by one of those painful doubts that I have known trouble your mind on more than one occasion.

Well, my friend, let's take a look at what God has to say about the possession of this life. And if you accept his testimony, as I know you do, and have done for a long time, he himself will convince you of a truth that your soul now prizes above all else. For the disciple of Jesus who waits till he is on his deathbed before he takes hold of the assurance of God's grace towards him is in a pitiable state indeed!

When it comes to passing into eternity, it requires more than a mere hope to comfort the soul. What brings comfort at such a time is rather the promise, clearly understood and firmly taken hold of, that 'Whoever believes in Christ has life by faith in his name.'

The Saviour's great love

Therefore, in order to understand it better, let us reflect for a moment on the great and sovereign love of God towards the church whom he has chosen and for whom Jesus gave his life as a ransom, that he might redeem them completely.

Understand, then, my dear friend, that the Saviour did not die in vain. His blood was truly shed for the remission of the sins of those for whom it was poured out. Contemplate for a moment the Son of God, come to us from the Father, in human flesh and effectually made one with his people. In this intimate union, he took on himself the sins of the elect and he bore in his own body the full force of the curse which should have fallen on them.

Consider how Christ, the Son of God, by himself, has certainly purged his people from their sins. He was delivered up for their offences, and he was raised again for their justification. Try to grasp the extent to which, when the Messiah was released from the crushing burden of condemnation and anguish, he saved and redeemed before God the people on whose behalf he had been broken. He did it as effectively as a benefactor who secures the release from prison of a debtor, by first assuming responsibility for his debt and then cancelling it by paying it in full.

Gaze, then, in wonder and adoration, on this sovereign love of God who loved those whom it pleased him to love. He was not content simply to invite them to be saved or to make salvation possible for them. No, he has actually saved and redeemed them in Jesus Christ, because, being one with them, Jesus himself passed through the hell and the condemnation that should have been theirs. He has given them his life, having taken their death on himself.

Oh, let us adore and worship such great love, for this really took place and his love is still the same today. Jesus is alive, and that after having tasted death for those who belong to him!

Why Christians doubt

I am stressing this point, because I am convinced that there can be no true grounds for peace for the soul based on any foundation other than this atoning death of the Son of God. Now, his death was not an atoning death if it took place for sins which, in the end, that is, at the last day, will be found to have not been atoned for.

This subject is often discussed, even among those who sincerely love the truth. However, we must always come back to this point: to consider the Saviour's sacrifice as having been offered on behalf of men who will finally be lost amounts in fact to completely annulling the atoning nature of this sacrifice. It is as if a sum of money were to be paid to discharge a debt, and yet that debt still could still remain outstanding. Is it possible that God could have paid us in false coin, so to speak?

I have seen evidence of this particular error in you. It is, in my opinion, one of the most perfidious heresies that can be advanced against the faith. And I believe it is the reason why the faith of so many Christians is faltering, uncertain, fearful and, consequently, fails to produce fruit in their lives. At least, that is what I have found in virtually every single case where disciples of the Lord who are not well-grounded in the faith have sought my advice.

I have always seen this false view that the Lord shed his blood for every individual member of the human race as the cause of their doubts and, consequently, of their fears. This view is always based in their thinking on a faulty interpretation of various passages of Scripture which do indeed speak of the inclusion of *all types* of men, or men of *every nation* on earth, among the people redeemed by the Lord. However, these passages never speak of the blood of the Lamb being shed for those who will not ultimately be purged from their sins. This blood, dear friend, has been shed for the remission of sins; so has it been shed for sins that will not in fact be forgiven?

It is not fitting that I should develop this point further. I have enough confidence in your faith, and your habit of thinking deeply about things, to be sure that the reminder of a few basic principles will suffice to convince you that the church, the chosen family, has been redeemed by the Redeemer and saved by the Saviour. In other words, the Son of God did not come to offer up his soul in order to *help* the sinner who is loved by God through grace. He gave his life in order to *be* eternal life and salvation for this sinner whom he has chosen to bless.

In view of this salvation that has been accomplished by the Saviour, I am not afraid to say to you, 'Rejoice in him; and as you are on the point of entering into the presence of his glory in heaven, thrill in joyful antici-pation of what you already possess by faith.' For this, dear friend, is the pledge which God himself has given to the elect of his sovereign love which was already theirs in Jesus Christ even before time began, and it is to this that the Holy Spirit bears witness.

Christ's sacrifice must be perfect

To begin with, one thing is certain: either you have not been redeemed by the Saviour, or you have been. The sacrifice of the Son of God was perfect, as well as unique. The whole of God's elect family, whom the Lord will place at his right hand on the last day, will have been redeemed by him. Not one of those whom the Father has given him, not one of the sheep whom he has known by name and for whom he gave his life, will be either lost or wandering astray on that day. We are, therefore, speaking of a salvation that has either already been accomplished by the Saviour, or else it never will be.

Do not be afraid to contemplate this alternative, for it is the truth, and truth never leads us astray: rather it sets us free, brings happiness and makes us holy. Satan knows that only too well. That is why he either hides the truth or fights against it. As for you, my brother, reflect upon this truth, and when you have known and believed, according to the Scriptures, that the Lord Jesus has indeed saved those for whom he was slain and for whom he bore the curse, then go on to believe what God says about the man who has believed on the name of the Son of God.

This is the essential point, and the source of comfort to your soul. First see and recognize as applying to you what God says of his elect. Then, be at peace and joyfully depart this earthly life for the dwelling-place which has been prepared for you from before the foundation of the world.

Of course, if I was addressing you as a man who did not yet know the way of God, or if you did not believe the Bible, then I would be speaking to you in a completely different way. I would not set out before your ignorance the knowledge enjoyed by those who are mature.

The work of the Spirit in the lives of the elect

But in your case we are concerned with comfort, assurance, being established in the faith, adoption and victory, and not with the rudiments of the gospel. I am therefore using to you the language which your spiritual state requires and, in order to bring about in your soul, through the Word of the Spirit of grace, the conviction that you need, I ask you, whether you do not in fact manifest the characteristics that the Spirit of the Lord produces in his elect.

'Which ones?' you may ask.

I reply that there are three, each distinct from the other and very easy to recognize.

The first is *the knowledge of your own sinful state,* and the way in which you yourself condemn, from the bottom of your heart, everything that is contrary to the holy will of God. In other words, don't you see yourself as a sinner before God, and are you not grieved at having done wrong?

The second is *your inner consciousness of being unable to free your soul from its burden of sin by any efforts of your own*, such as good resolutions, tears, promises or sacrifices. To put it another way, haven't you given up trying to justify yourself before God? Don't you confess that if God dealt with you as you deserve, you would be justly condemned and banished from his presence?

The third is *the knowledge of the Lord Jesus, and faith in him*: that he is the Son of God, come from the Father, that he loved the church and redeemed it, and that salvation is only to be found in him and through him. Add to that faith in him, the submission of mind and heart to his great name, the reliance of the soul on his sacrifice and belief in this atonement made by the Saviour's blood for all the sins of his people. By that I mean, don't you believe, deep down in your heart, that Jesus truly came from God, that he truly lived among men, that he truly took upon himself the sins of the church, that he was raised by the glory of the Father and that he is now in heaven, whence he will return? Don't you believe in him? Doesn't your soul look to him, finally and sincerely, for forgiveness? Isn't your only plea the sacrifice of the Lamb (or at least you long that it should it be for you)? Isn't this what you believe?

84

I am sure that this is what you have received from God. I have heard you say so more than once. Isn't it true that you believe that you are a ruined sinner, and that you believe in the name of the Lord Jesus? Now, dear friend, such a belief is the gift of God to his elect. It is he who not only first grants to us the consciousness of our sin, and enables us to abandon any claim to a righteousness of our own, but also at the same time reveals to us that Jesus is the Son of God, the Christ, and grants us faith in him as our Saviour. This belief is the Christian faith, the faith of God's elect.

Then God goes on to declare that the soul that has received him and, after careful probing and self-examination, finds evidence within of such faith, is indwelt by Christ and therefore possesses life for, 'He who has the Son [of God] has life.' This means that God draws to the Son those whom the Son has redeemed, and he reveals this love to them by the faith which he gives them in Jesus.

Truth is truth

'But what about the fruits?' I think you will be asking me in your heart. 'Should the fruits of faith not be evident when there is faith in the soul? How, then, can I convince myself that the Lord Jesus dwells in me, when I cannot see in myself the things which should accompany his presence?'

'But,' I reply once more, 'if it is your doubt concerning the promise of God that prevents these fruits from appearing, then what must you first do if you want to produce them?'

'Take away the doubt,' you reply.

Yes, my dear friend. In other words, you must banish any thought of your own righteousness, which is always at the root of this doubt and keeps it alive. In fact, this doubt is really saying, '*I am not worthy* of being loved, justified or saved.' That is why I am not afraid to state that there is never any doubt about the perfect salvation that God has given us in his Son in any soul that has truly renounced all righteousness of its own, all self-seeking and all pursuit of its own worthiness.

And in any case, you must believe God. You are therefore left with this alternative: either you deny that you are a sinner, condemned because of what you have done, and that Jesus came to us from the Father to save the church; or else you deny that the one who has faith in God's Son has life. But God's gracious Word states that both these things are true. Therefore you must deny the Word of God before you can convince yourself that you are not saved; there is no other option left open to you.

Do you believe God's Word? Do you find in your heart faith in the testimony which God has given about his Son? If you do find it there, then you may know that you have eternal life: the two statements go together. 'He who has the Son has life,' God tells us.

On the other hand, if you say, 'No, I don't have life; I am not sure that I have it, because I can't feel it in me', then God's Word asks you if a reliable testimony is valid in and of itself because it is inherently true, or if it is only true in the opinion of the person who hears it and in the feelings of the person whom it concerns. Suppose a witness claims to have seen a man steal something before his very eyes, but the accused man is very unhappy about this evidence. Does it follow that the witness's evidence is unreliable, false even? Must the guilty man say that he is pleased to hear it for it to be true?

In the same way, a reliable witness, the Lord himself, states that you are robbing him of his glory by attributing some worthiness to yourself. He declares that all the glory belongs to him, and to him alone; salvation is a gift of his grace and is to the praise of his glory. Your heart does not like this evidence, accustomed as it is to the theft of which it is accused, and it rejects the evidence with all kinds of subterfuges and excuses. Does this rejection invalidate the testimony of God, or does your denial make the charge any less true? He says, eternal life is a gift of God in Jesus. Is what he says true, or not?

A question of fruitfulness

'But', you reply with a groan, 'can this be true for me, even though I do not bear any fruit?' It is true in itself, but you do not believe it for what it is. You doubt it, and that is your real trouble, the principal point where you have gone wrong. And then, when you became aware of the lack of fruit in your life, what did you do to try to put things right? I am going to tell you.

Because your lack of fruit appeared to indicate a lack of faith, you thought that you needed to bear fruit in order to prove to yourself that you did have faith. By this false reasoning, you have kept your soul bound up with its own righteousness, preoccupied with yourself and your works. This has led you more and more to forget the testimony and promises of God and you have become attached to duties rather than to Jesus. The result is even more doubts which have only made the problem worse by confirming you in your unbelief.

Would you have done the same thing if you had been looking after a tree? Suppose you had noticed that it failed to produce fruit. Would you have said, 'I must do something to the branches to make them bear more fruit?' Wouldn't you rather have said, 'The life-bearing sap has stopped flowing. I must do something about the root and the trunk of the tree. The branches depend on them. If the sap is flowing freely, the fruit will follow'?

That is exactly what you must do for the tree that is your soul. Has its fruit been sparse and of poor quality? That is caused by a lack of sap. Therefore you must concentrate on the sap, that is, the Spirit of God, who is given to the true disciple who has faith. So you must begin by believing God when he speaks to you of his love in Jesus. Believe him when he makes you a promise; believe that promise — what it actually states and all that it implies — and, having believed, you will grow.

The same is true for the soul as for the tree. The latter grows when the sap flows in abundance; similarly, the soul grows and bears fruit when faith abounds. 'The one who believes grows,' should be the Christian's motto in the garden of the Lord where he is planted. When he does not produce much fruit, he must remember to tend immediately, not the branches of the tree, but the roots. He must return once more to Jesus, gaze upon him, listen to him, believe him and rest in complete confidence on his promises; and then (and never until then) he will produce the fruits of peace, assurance (that is, of adoption), joy, true repentance, true watchfulness and a sure and certain hope, based on the Lord's own word, of true, living, heavenly immortality.

Faith sees only the grace of God

I therefore conclude that you have no grounds for rejecting God's promise simply because you are still dissatisfied with yourself. What you need is to be fully satisfied with God. That is all he requires of you and all that is expected of you. This dissatisfaction with yourself comes from your doubts about the validity of his promise. So you must begin by believing his promise and then, in the joy of faith and in the certainty that God has had mercy on you and loves you, as you take great delight in him, rejoice in him and worship him for his great love, you will find that you become, not satisfied with yourself, but content to remain dissatisfied.

I mean that you will come to regard the sight and the consciousness of your corrupt nature as a precious lesson that God is teaching you. Even as he reveals to you, as a child whom he has received and pardoned, just how greatly you have offended against him, in the light of his grace, you will be reminded by that very discovery that it is by grace alone that you are alive at all. Then, too, the same Spirit of grace and peace will teach you to put away all that belongs to your corrupt nature, not in any sense of discouragement or annoyance, but as something that is beneath you, over which you have gained the victory, as befits one whom Christ has redeemed.

In a word, my friend, abide in grace and you will be sanctified. Abide in Christ and you will be obedient. Take hold of the tree of life and you will eat its fruit. Believe, oh! believe what God tells you and the fruit of his Spirit will be seen in your life as you seek to follow the example of your God, whom that same Spirit will teach you to call 'Father'.

This, then, my dear friend, is the way you need to prepare for your solemn entrance into eternity; and it is with this assurance, given to you from on high through the gracious word of the Father in Jesus, that your soul should seek to fulfil the last of its duties here below and that you should spend your final moments of watching and waiting for the Lord. It is in this assurance, in simple faith and a spirit of humility and submission, yet at the same time confident, exultant, as one who is more than a conqueror, that you are to look forward to the moment when your spirit will leave your body here below, to enter into that infinite existence that we can only know in the measure that God has revealed it to us.

Jesus is already there, and that should be enough for us. And when we speak of Jesus, we speak of God's gift of love. Who would be afraid of appearing before a God of love? Does he only half love us? Does he love without really loving — in other words, in word only?

This everlasting life into which we enter, which stretches out beyond the grave, is the dwelling-place of God himself. It is filled with God's presence. What joy it is, then, for the soul of one who desires only God, who has no righteousness or life except in God and seeks only the presence and the faithfulness of God, to be brought, all at once, into possession of such a treasure!

Once again, this treasure is the gift of God's grace. And it is to be found in our glorious Lord and Saviour, Jesus Christ. This treasure is life; and whoever has Christ, has life. To have Christ means to believe on him.

To believe on him means to renounce all righteousness of one's own and to rest wholly, from the heart, on the Son of God and his work on our behalf.

It is, then, in such faith (a wonderful and gracious gift of the Father to his elect!) that your soul, dear friend, will continue in the work of obedience that God requires of you today and that the Spirit of adoption will sustain your soul, by granting you the patience that waits on God and blesses his name.

The blood of Christ cleanses us from all sin

It is as one who has been saved, as a sinner washed in the blood of the Lamb, that you are going to finish the course, in which the goal and the prize are entrance into God's rest, according to the infinite riches of his kindness. Your soul, taught by the truth, sees your sins as red like crimson. Well, so they may be, but the blood of Jesus, poured out when he bore the condemnation of God, is a red of an even deeper dye. The stain of your guilt is absorbed into the blood flowing from the cross of shame. Your soul emerges washed as white as snow. You remember all your sins, all your faults, all your rebellious acts, only in order to set against them grace — the infinite grace of God. This causes you to glorify the mercy of the Lord, falling down before him and shedding tears of contrition and gratitude.

The sinful woman weeps at the feet of the Saviour, but her sobs are not those of grief and desolation. She loves him; that is why she sheds so many tears. She is relieved of the crushing weight of so much immorality, so many sins. For that very reason, in wonder at such mercy, and because she knows at what great cost this blessing was obtained, she humbles her soul in worship and affection. Oh, happy woman, who heard the voice of the Saviour say, 'Go in peace!' Oh, happy indeed was the sinner whose love was all the greater for having been forgiven so much!

We too can know this blessing: we have the same inheritance; his love is one and the same. Christ is the same today as he was then. He is still just as full of love, faithfulness and power. Our High Priest is always ready to have compassion on his poor, fickle disciples who are so prone to temptation, and he will never turn his back on the sheep who tries to run away. On the contrary, he calls it back, goes after it, takes it in his arms and brings it back to the fold.

That is the love in which you must abide, my friend! No more doubts — none at all! The mouth of the Lord has spoken, and his testimony is sure. Resist everything which tells you otherwise. Listen to the Word of the gospel of grace, and silence all other voices. It is the voice of God that you need to hear now.

Let the world, your human reasoning, everything both within and around you, keep silence, so that Jesus alone may remain, and his gracious voice can give you the assurance, as your soul waits quietly and humbly for him to speak, that in him is to be found cleansing from every sin. Let this voice reassure you that he came for that very reason, so that even the very worst of sinners might receive complete and eternal forgiveness for all their transgressions, by faith in the name and the blood of the one beloved of the Father.

He himself will do it, for he is near you. He is 'wonderful in counsel and excellent in guidance'. Even now, as you read what your brother has written about his love, his eyes are on you. Surely he is waiting to answer, 'Here I am!' the very moment that you turn towards him with that first faint whisper of trust in him! When has he ever turned a sinner away? When has the humblest wretch who sought him ever been put to shame?

And so, I now commit and refer you to him, by his word of forgiveness and life. What a privilege is yours! If you suffer, it is under his watchful eye, so that you might obey him, and he is at hand to give you courage. If you feel the world slipping away from you and if your flesh is conscious of weakness and decay, Jesus is there, telling you, 'I am the resurrection and the life. He who believes in me, though he may die, he shall live.'

When the time comes for you to leave this earthly life for eternity, you may, in your suffering, still tremble and fear, but Jesus will be there with his rod and his staff. He will remind you that it is because of him, clothed in him and by the grace of the Father in him, that you are entering into everlasting life, so that you may for all eternity gladly owe everything to him and rejoice that you have been saved by him at such great cost.

Yes, my friend, that is what the Spirit of faith, the Spirit of God and Comforter of the church, will accomplish. Seek him, ask for him and, above all, listen to him and follow him. His is a gentle voice that speaks in our hearts and always in accordance with what is written. Hold fast, then, in great humility and affection, to the Word of your God.

So may your soul, delivered at last from its sinful flesh and from the doubts, conflicts, temptations and unfaithfulness of that miserable state, depart, happy and blessed, to appear before the one who created it pure and who redeemed it from its ruined state in order to glorify it in himself in that abode of his grace and the rest that he gives.

And so, farewell, dear friend! Farewell! Soon I, too, will be standing on the threshold about to leave this earthly, mortal life. Soon I, too, washed like you in the blood of Jesus, will depart to be with him and to fall down at his feet and join you for all eternity in giving the love and adoration that is due to the Lord our God — Father, Son and Holy Spirit!

An anecdote from Ireland

A few days after I had written the 'Letter to a friend', I learnt that my friend had departed this life for his eternal homeland. I said in that letter that the reason why so many Christians are uncertain about their own salvation is always a false view of the extent of the Saviour's atoning work. I could quote many facts and the testimony of many witnesses in support of this assertion, but for the present I will confine myself to a report of the following incident, which I will try to recount as faithfully as possible.

An anecdote from Ireland

I was on a visit to the north of Ireland and I heard people talk about the piety of an old man who lived up in the mountains. I wanted to make his acquaintance for myself and so I made my way to his poor hut, made of clay and situated on a hill in a wild and very bleak spot.

Old Joseph was by himself when I appeared at his door. I found him seated in a kind of room which contained only the barest necessities in the way of furniture. Everything about this dwelling proclaimed the most extreme poverty. The old man's clothing also reflected this state of utter destitution.

This dear Christian welcomed me in a serious manner, but also very gently. He immediately entered into a conversation with me about 'the true riches, the treasure that neither moth nor rust can corrupt — about the grace of God in our Saviour Jesus'.

'Soon,' I said to Joseph, you will be leaving this life

of poverty and pain to take possession of these heavenly treasures.'

'I already possess them by faith,' he replied calmly but clearly, 'and I expect to see them any day now. I have always known very great poverty here below. You can see my home for yourself. There is nothing in that chest, nothing in this cupboard and when I die my children will not find enough here to bury their father. But, since the Lord has revealed his grace to me, I have been very rich. It is now nearly fifty years since I received this blessing which makes me happier with every day that passes. What a joy it is for me to see the end of my journey approaching and to have the assurance that I shall be welcome in the presence of my God, who has given me eternal life in his holy Son!'

Joseph then told me that one of his sons, who lived a little higher up the mountain, was also a disciple of the Saviour. At my request to visit him, Joseph got up and led me up the path which led to the cottage of his son Daniel.

The son's home was no wealthier than his father's. When we entered, he was sitting by the fire, with two young boys beside him, and talking to his wife who was nursing a third child.

Joseph told him who I was and I was received, in the words of the apostle Paul, 'like an angel from heaven'. Daniel got up and came to take my hand between his in a gesture of respect as he said, 'May the Lord bless the entrance of his servant into my humble dwelling!'

This prayer was truly answered, for this is what happened. I had asked Daniel and his wife a few questions about their children and, in particular, I had asked the father if he was bringing them up in the grace and under the watchful eye of the Lord Jesus, their Good Shepherd.

'As far as I can!' replied Daniel with a sigh. He was standing up, leaning against the post of the open door, and his whole manner was that of a man weighed down with cares and sorrows.

'I take it, Daniel,' I said to him, 'that you have experienced this grace and you have no doubts about your own salvation?'

Daniel crossed his arms on his chest and, with an even deeper sigh, he stared silently at the ground, for there was no floor in his hut. I repeated my question and the words, 'Sometimes ... not always ... at the moment not at all!' were the only answer I received.

'Tell me, Daniel,' I continued, 'aren't you convinced of your sinful state before God?'

'Oh, miserable wretch that I am!' he replied with feeling. 'There is no sinner like me. I am nothing but sin and defilement.'

'And that grieves you, from what I can see?'

'Not as much as it should. Yet God knows that I often weep before him over my sinfulness. Oh, I am only a miserable wretch, a guilty rebel!'

'And,' I asked him, 'you don't think that you can earn or deserve forgiveness for yourself?'

He answered me in a low voice, as if he was reproaching me, 'I will never deny the Lord Jesus. It is he, and not I, who blots out sins.'

'Why are you so sad, then, Daniel? Hasn't the blood been shed that takes away the guilt and defilement of our souls and hasn't the Saviour offered a complete and perfect sacrifice?'

'I believe that with all my heart,' he replied, 'but ... I sometimes wonder if I shall not finally be rejected. For in the end, all will not go to heaven, although the sacrifice was offered for all!'

So that was what was troubling this soul. Daniel had not yet understood that the Saviour had, by his death, actually purged the sins of his people. He considered the sacrifice of the Son of God as being of indeterminate extent, as an act of kindness on behalf of the human race in general, but of no one in particular. Since this sacrifice had, as he thought, been made for Judas Iscariot, as well as for every man, and yet Judas was the son of perdition, so he had reason to fear the same destiny for himself in the end.

I wanted to know, above all, the passages of Scripture on which he based his opinion. He first said to me, 'Didn't the Lord Jesus say that God loved *the world* when he gave his only begotten Son?'

'Daniel,' I answered, 'to whom was the Lord Jesus talking when he said that?'

'To Nicodemus, who was a teacher of the Jews,' he replied.

'Did the Jews in general believe that salvation would be for all nations?'

'I think not,' he admitted. 'On the contrary, they thought that only the Jewish nation would be blessed.'

'And was it only to the Jewish nation that Jesus was sent by the Father?'

'Old Simeon says that the salvation of God was to be a light to all peoples.'

'So you see,' I answered, 'why the Saviour told Nicodemus that God now includes the world, and not just one nation, in the gospel age. So this passage simply means what the apostle Paul says elsewhere in writing to Timothy, namely that God wants salvation to come to and be proclaimed to *all men*. It is for that very reason that he, Paul, was made "a preacher ... and a teacher of the Gentiles", that is, of the nations of the world.'

'That is very clear, Daniel,' Joseph interrupted affectionately. 'Can't you see it?'

'Yes, father,' replied the son in a very respectful tone, 'and thank you for explaining it. I hadn't understood the passage in that sense... But, all the same, doesn't John the Baptist speak of the Lord Jesus as "the Lamb of God who takes away the sin of the world"?'

I looked at Joseph to see if he wanted to answer himself. The old man nodded, indicating that I should speak, so I said, 'Do you think, Daniel, that the lamb offered at Passover could take away the sin of those who offered it?'

'The blood of bulls and goats could not purge the conscience of the sinner,' he replied, 'and nor could that of a lamb.'

'But the blood of the Lamb of God could do so, couldn't it? So it was fitting that the forerunner, pointing to the Lord Jesus, should say, "This is the true Lamb whom the Passover lamb served only to foreshadow. It is he who actually takes away sins, something that the other could not do." At the same time, John the Baptist was showing that the Lord was sent to the whole world, and not just to one nation.'

The father looked once more at his son, as if to ask if he understood. But Daniel, opening his Bible and putting his finger on a passage, said once more, 'However, the apostle John declares that "He is the propitiation for our sins, and not for ours only but also for those of the whole world"' (1 John 2:2).

'It is that version you have there which says that, Daniel. The original text does not say that.'

'Is that true?' his father intervened. 'What does it say, then, please? For I must admit this passage has puzzled me. I have often tried to understand what it meant and it still isn't clear to me.'

'First of all,' I answered, 'you will notice that the apostle John is writing to converted Jews, because he says to them in verse 7 that they have had the "old commandment ... from the beginning". Now, the Gentiles had never had the law of God. It was the Hebrew nation that had it.'

'I had never seen that,' Joseph remarked, 'but I can see it very clearly now.'

'It is equally clear, as you will see,' I continued, that the apostle is speaking in this way to his own people, his compatriots, and telling them that the Saviour is a Saviour, not only for the Jews, but also for all the world. "He is," he says, "the propitiation for our sins, and not for *ours* only" (that is, for our nation, our fellow-citizens), "but also for *the whole world.*"

'But it says, "for *the sins* of the whole world",' exclaimed the son.

'No, my dear Daniel. These two words, "the sins", are not in the original text, which says only, "for the whole world". And to convince you of what I am saying, look at the comment made by the same apostle on the prophecy of the high priest Caiaphas (John 11:51-52). "Jesus", he says, "would die for the nation, and not for that nation only, but also that he would gather together in one the children of God who were scattered abroad," in other words, for the whole world.'

'Thank you very much!' exclaimed Joseph. 'Praise God! That really sheds light on it for me. So all this passage is concerned with is the fact that the "wall of separation" between Jews and Gentiles has been taken away by the Saviour's coming, which is proclaimed to the whole world, and not just to one nation… Can you see that, too, Daniel?'

Daniel put his Bible down and taking up his former stance once more, remained silent, with head bent and a troubled expression.

'As far as I can see,' I went on, 'it is the same with all the other passages which appear to say that the Saviour was slain for the whole human race. If you study them carefully, you see that there is not one of them, not a single one, that teaches that.

'All Scripture, as it bears testimony to Jesus, says and affirms what he himself declared: it is for "his sheep", that is, for those whom the Father has given him, that he laid down his life. He is the Head of the church which is his body, the Bridegroom of the bride. He did not offer up his soul as a sacrifice on behalf of souls for whom he did not pray when he was preparing for his sacrifice.'

Daniel repeated in a low voice: 'I do not pray for the world…' (John 17:9), and sighed deeply.

'So, dear Daniel,' I continued, 'I declare that according to this truth, which is the truth of God, if you are one of those for whom the Lamb was slain, your salvation is not something that still has to be accomplished. No, it has already been accomplished, once and for all, by the Saviour.'

'And if I am not one of them?' Daniel asked quietly.

'I say that if God declares that you are one of them, you must believe him. Indeed, "He who does not believe the testimony that God has given has made him a liar." Now if God has loved you, Daniel, in his holy Son Jesus, it is God who must tell you so. If you believe his testimony, you will have peace.'

I then explained in detail the gospel of grace. I showed how the Father has given eternal life in Jesus Christ to those sinners whom it has pleased him to save. I spoke of the way in which the Son of God, having loved this church that the Father has given him, gave himself for it and saved it, in himself, perfectly and for ever. I explained how the Holy Spirit, who has made the church one with the Saviour, reveals this grace to the children of men who have been the objects of it and seals it to their hearts.

I showed how it is the Father who, by various means appointed by his wisdom and love, draws to the Lord Jesus the elect sinner (who is as yet unaware of his election). I told them how it is also the Father who reveals Jesus to the sinner and, by his Word and by the Holy Spirit, creates faith in him, that is, the belief of the heart in the name of Jesus Christ. Finally I showed how the soul to whom it has been granted to believe in that name should have assurance that it possesses eternal life. 'For, ultimately,' I added, by way of a conclusion, '"If we receive the witness of men, the witness of God is greater," as the apostle John tells us' (1 John 5:9).

'But,' Daniel resumed quietly, as if he was afraid of in some way contradicting the Word of God, 'if I do not see in myself the evidence ... the results of ... what God has said, do I have the right to believe it?'

'I would like you to listen to the account of an incident which I was told about by reliable witnesses only a few days after it took place. It will show you what it means to take someone at his word when the speaker is trustworthy. The Emperor Napoleon was reviewing a regiment in front of his palace, in Paris. As he was giving his orders, he let go of the reins of his horse, which immediately ran off. A simple soldier of the line, a very agile man, leaped in front of the horse, skilfully seized hold of the bridle and gave it back to the emperor, who said to him, "Much obliged, captain!" "What regiment, sir?" asked the soldier. "My guards," answered the commander, who set off at a gallop.

'So the soldier is left standing in the middle of the square, but he is not there by himself: he has the monarch's word, and he trusts it. So, even though he is still only wearing the uniform of a rifleman, and still has his weapon in his hand, he considers himself to be more than a simple soldier. Putting down his rifle, he turns, not to his place in the line, but to the staff headquarters and goes up to it.

'"What's this man doing, coming here?" asks one of the generals. "This man," he replies confidently, "is captain of the guards." "You!" someone says. "Yes, because *he* said so," he replies, pointing to the emperor. "Oh, sir!" comes the respectful answer, "I am sorry, I didn't know."

'Yet you see, Daniel, this soldier wasn't dressed as a captain; he didn't have any epaulettes or a sword, and yet...'

'Ah!' Joseph quickly broke in. 'But he had something better than that. The sovereign's word was worth more than a uniform.'

'Yes, Joseph,' I answered seriously, 'much more. This man honoured the word of another man who could not lie to him. He received immediately, in his heart, the assurance and the enjoyment of what he had just been promised.'

Joseph looked at his son. 'He did for his king what Abraham had done for his God. Abraham, too, relied on what the Lord God had said, and he was assured that it would be as the Lord had promised' (Rom. 4:20-21).

'If it was you, Daniel,' I went on, 'you might have said, "When I have my epaulettes, then I will believe I am a captain, but not before."'

Daniel didn't answer. He remained standing, leaning against the doorpost. He was weeping silently, but so copiously that the ground at his feet was wet and glistening. Joseph was also keenly interested. His hands were clasped and he was watching his son with an expression of tender concern. Daniel's wife, with her infant sleeping on her lap and her arms around her two other children, was listening intently. It seemed to me that the Lord was looking on us graciously and blessing us.

He was also blessing Daniel and setting him free, applying to his soul, little by little, by means of the Spirit of adoption, the blessed and powerful assurance of his salvation.

'You understand,' I went on, 'that to doubt when the Lord declares something to be case is to turn away from the testimony that God has given to look at oneself. If, when God tells you that "He who believes in the Son has everlasting life," you answer, "I am sure that I believe in the Son, but I am still not sure if I have life," this answer is an insult to God. It is as if you were to say that his word is not enough for you and that you need more reliable evidence to convince you. So, in fact, you are giving less honour to God than the soldier gave to a man.'

Daniel clasped his hands together tightly and his tears flowed even more freely and turned to sobs. I then said to him, 'So you see, Daniel, that since you believe in your heart in the name of the Lord Jesus Christ, you should also believe that you have received that faith from the Father himself, for he alone gives it. You should also know, as John tells us, that you have eternal life, even now (1 John 5:13). Tell me, doesn't such a promise, such an assurance, fill you with joy?'

'I am ashamed before the Lord,' Daniel replied solemnly, 'that up till now I have been making God a liar' (1 John 5:10).

Such was his answer. This dear Christian had just understood that the witness of God must be believed because it is the truth, and that the doubts he had cherished until then were sins of pride and self-righteousness which had caused him to reject the promise of God to rely instead on the feelings of his own heart.

Daniel then went on to speak as a man whom the truth had just made free. He raised his head and grew calm. He told us how relieved and happy he was. 'I had a continual burden on my heart,' he said, 'and I only rarely enjoyed the presence of God. Sometimes I thought I was saved but, more often than not, I was filled with fear. When I prayed to God, it always seemed to me that I did not have full access to his throne and when I had sinned, I was afraid of him and did not dare to appear before his face.'

I asked him in what spirit he tried to obey the commands of God. He answered, 'Oh, now, I feel it will be entirely different. Since God has *told me*' (he emphasized these two words) 'that I am one of his children, it will be as one of his children that I shall seek to obey him.

'It is totally different — totally different!' he repeated. 'Indeed it is. I can see it now. Up till now, I had always thought that I believed the Bible. But what I believed was really my own ideas. *Now,* I believe what God says. The Bible is true and what God says is a fact; that is why I rely upon it. May his holy name be blessed!'

So deliverance came at last to this poor soul, who had been led astray by a lie and who would never have known rest if the Father had not revealed to him all the Lord Jesus is, and had not enabled him, by his Spirit, to believe this promise: 'He who believes on the Son has everlasting life.'

As we were going back down the path, Joseph said to me, 'I am amazed that Daniel has been so long in doubt. For, after all, the testimony of God is very simple and clear.'

'It is the Lord who opens,' I replied, 'as it is he who closes. To him be all the glory, in all things!'